WRESTLING
is for me

WRESTLING
is for me

text and photographs by
Art Thomas

 Lerner Publications Company   Minneapolis

The author wishes to thank Andy Garcia and his parents; the members of the Brooklyn Y.M.C.A. Wrestling Club and their parents; Dave Garcia, who contributed many of the ideas for the book; and Carl Badger, who helped with the photography.

To my teachers, who have taught me much through the years

LIBRARY OF CONGRESS CATALOGING IN PUBLICATION DATA

Thomas, Art.
Wrestling is for me.

(The Sports for Me Books)
SUMMARY: Twelve-year-old Andy tells of his first year of wrestling during which he learns, with the help of his coach, the various moves and becomes ready to wrestle in a tournament.

1. Wrestling—Juvenile literature. [1. Wrestling] I. Title. II. Series.

GV1195.T465 1979   796.8'12   79-1487
ISBN 0-8225-1085-5

Manufactured in the United States of America.
Published simultaneously in Canada by J. M. Dent & Sons (Canada) Ltd., Don Mills, Ontario.

International Standard Book Number: 0-8225-1085-5
Library of Congress Catalog Card Number: 79-1487

1 2 3 4 5 6 7 8 9 10 85 84 83 82 81 80 79

Hi! My name is Andy, and I'm 12 years old. I like lots of sports. But my favorite sport is wrestling. I've learned that it takes a lot of work and practice, but that it's fun, too. Even though I don't know everything about wrestling yet, I would like to tell you what it was like getting started in the sport.

For as long as I can remember, the boys who live in my neighborhood have wrestled in their yards. We were not mad at each other. Wrestling was a way of having fun.

One of the boys in the neighborhood was Darryl. He was in a wrestling program at his high school. Darryl told me that sport wrestling was different from the kind of wrestling we did in our yards. He said that sport wrestlers must follow rules. In a wrestling match, two wrestlers have three one-minute periods to try to **pin** each other. To pin an opponent, a wrestler must hold the opponent's shoulder blades on the mat for at least two seconds.

If neither wrestler can pin his opponent, the one with the most points wins the match. Wrestlers are awarded points during the match for special moves.

Darryl said that I could see sport wrestling at his school's next **meet**, or wrestling competition. I asked my parents if they would take me, and they said yes. Dad told me that it would not be anything like "big time" wrestling on television. The high school wrestlers, for example, would not be in a ring. They would wrestle on a special foam mat so they would not get hurt.

I was surprised to see so many people at
the school watching the wrestling matches.
There were boys and girls my age, older
kids, and grownups, too.

I noticed that when the boys wrestled, they moved really fast. They seemed to know many different holds and special ways to get out of these holds. When one move did not work, the wrestlers quickly tried something else.

A referee in a black and white shirt watched each match carefully. I did not understand the scoring yet, but the referee sure did. He gave points to boys who performed certain moves. The referee also made sure that the wrestlers followed the rules so no one got hurt.

Darryl won his match. Everyone clapped because it was so exciting. I decided then that I would like to learn wrestling. I wanted to be as good as Darryl was.

Dad said that my school had a wrestling program for boys my age. He took me there the next day so that I could meet the coach and the other boys who were interested in wrestling.

I felt funny at the first practice. All of the other boys had had experience in wrestling. Almost all of them were wearing a **singlet**. A singlet is a uniform that wrestlers wear. I was wearing a regular tee shirt and shorts. But Coach Arnold said my gym clothes were just fine for practice. So I didn't care.

We started practice with some warm-up exercises. First we stretched all the muscles in our arms and legs. I couldn't stretch nearly as far as the other boys could.

We also did exercises to build up our muscles. Mr. Arnold said that this conditioning was important because wrestlers use every muscle in their bodies.

The other boys weren't as tired as I was after the exercises. But they told me not to worry. If I exercised every day, I would soon be in shape like they were.

When we started wrestling, I thought I would be as good as many of the boys there. I wasn't. Everything they showed me was new. I had to practice every new move step by step.

The first thing I learned was a **stance**, or special way of standing. This is the stance that begins every match. You stand with your feet spread apart and your knees slightly bent. Hold your hands out, but keep your elbows in at your sides. The boys kept reminding me to keep my head up and to be ready to wrestle.

Next I learned the **referee's position**. This is the way wrestlers begin the second and third periods of every match. The wrestler on top has the "advantage." This means that he is in a better position of control. The top man has one hand on his opponent's belly button. The other hand holds his opponent's elbow. The man on the bottom is on his hands and knees. His weight is spread evenly.

Both wrestlers watch the referee for the signal to begin the period. There are lots of moves the wrestlers can try once the period begins.

The top man in the referee's position must try to keep control of the bottom man. The easiest way to do this is to put the bottom man off balance so that he is flat on his stomach rather than on his hands and knees.

You can try a **breakdown** to make your opponent fall. Pull in on his left elbow with your left hand. At the same time, push forward into him with your legs and body. To help yourself keep control, grab your opponent's left wrist with both of your hands. This move is called a **double wrist ride** or **two on one**.

The bottom man in the referee's position should try several moves to gain points. Some moves are called **escapes**. In an escape, the bottom man breaks completely away from the top man's control. A successful escape is worth one point.

One escape is the **stand-up**. From the referee's position, quickly put your outside

foot flat on the mat in front of you. At
the same time, arch your back and neck.
With one hand, pull your opponent's wrist
back and away from your chest. Sweep
your other arm back to prevent him from
grabbing your ankle. Quickly stand up on
both feet. Then step forward, and turn to
face your opponent.

The bottom man in the referee's position can also do a move called a **switch**. It is started by crossing your left hand in front of your right so your opponent can't pull it back. At the same time, you must lift your right knee a few inches off the mat.

The next step is to swing your left leg underneath your body to the other side. When you do this, your entire body will turn around. You will now be outside your opponent's control.

Since your opponent's hand is still around your waist, reach your right hand inside his right leg. Keeping your neck straight, arch your body toward him without pushing into him. Then kick your left leg over your opponent, completing the move. You will have gone from the bottom to the top. This is called a **reversal**. Whenever a wrestler does a reversal, he is awarded two points.

23

Another wrestling move is called a **takedown**. A takedown begins with both wrestlers standing. Then one of them performs a move that puts him in a position of advantage. Whenever a wrestler does a successful takedown, he is awarded two points.

I learned how to do a **single leg takedown**. You start the move by dropping in front of your opponent, landing on one knee. You must be sure to land very close to him. If you are reaching for his right leg, as I am here, your right hand should be at his knee and your left hand behind his shoe.

Next you must push against your opponent with your head and shoulder. At the same time, pull in at his ankle. This will make your opponent fall backward on the mat.

To complete the takedown, move on top of your opponent. Keep in control by holding onto his legs or arm.

Escapes, reversals, and takedowns are all good moves for gaining points. But the real goal of wrestling is to win by a **fall**, or pin. Then points do not matter. Every good wrestler should know at least one good pinning move. I learned the **half nelson**.

To do a half nelson, slide one arm under your opponent's arm and place both hands on the back of his head. You can then turn him over easily.

When your opponent is on his back, you can work for a pin. Keep your hand tightly around his head and balance your weight over him. Looking up while you do this will cause your chest to weigh more heavily on your opponent. If his shoulder blades touch the mat for two seconds, the referee will signal a pin.

There was a lot more to wrestling than I had first thought. There were so many moves to remember. Coach Arnold said that if I practiced each move over and over, I would get better at it.

Boy, was I sore the next morning! Dad said the stiffness would soon go away. He said I was sore because I had used muscles for wrestling that I normally do not use much.

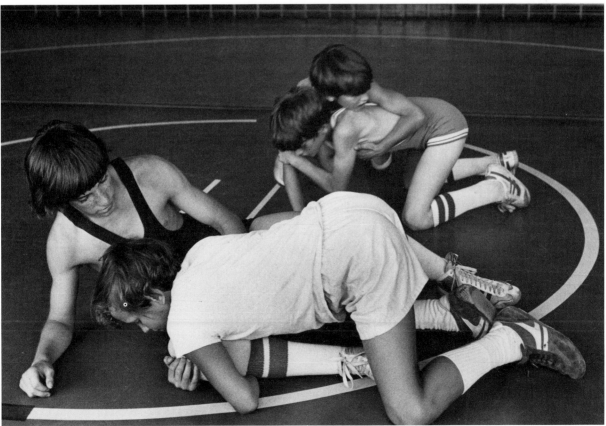

After a few weeks of practice, I was not getting sore anymore. The practices were hard, but I didn't mind. I learned more each day. My moves were getting better and better.

One day at practice, Mr. Arnold asked me if I wanted to wrestle for the team in their last meet of the season. One of the wrestlers was going on a trip, and the team needed someone to fill in for him.

Of course I wanted to wrestle in a real meet. But I was worried, too. I was afraid I didn't know enough about wrestling to win. But Mr. Arnold said that it didn't matter how many different moves I knew. It was more important to be able to do a few moves really well.

On the day of the meet, I was nervous. There were 12 members on our team, and I was the only one who had not wrestled before. The matches started with the lightest wrestlers at 80 pounds and went up to the heaviest at 175 pounds. I weighed 90 pounds and would wrestle third.

In my match, I used many of the moves that I had learned in practice. But my opponent seemed stronger than I was. I was very tired by the end of the second period.

In the last period, I got pinned. I worked as hard as I could, but my opponent was more experienced than I was. The referee saw that my shoulder blades were on the mat and signalled a pin by slapping his hand on the mat.

After the match, I shook hands with my opponent. Then my teammates came onto the mat to meet me. I couldn't look at them. I had lost and let the team down. I started crying.

Everyone tried to cheer me up. They said that the important thing was that I tried my hardest. They said that I would have other chances to wrestle, and that each time I would get better.

So I stopped feeling bad and began to cheer for the other wrestlers on our team. Our team won the meet, even though I had lost my match. In wrestling, the team gets three points for every wrestler who wins his match by having more points than his opponent. The team gets six points for every wrestler who wins by a pin. Because our team had many good wrestlers, we won more matches and won the meet.

There were only a few more weeks of practice left before the big tournament at the end of the season. In the tournament, each wrestler would enter as an individual. There would be no team scores in this tournament. Once you lost, you would be out of the running for a trophy.

Mr. Arnold and my teammates helped me practice for the tournament. They showed me some things I had done wrong in my first match. I was not keeping my back straight when I went in for a takedown. I worked on correcting my mistakes before they became habits. I kept getting better.

My parents knew how much I was looking forward to the tournament. They seemed just as excited as I was. The day of the tournament, they had a surprise for me. They had bought me my very own singlet. I couldn't wait to wear it in my first match.

There were over 300 wrestlers in the tournament. We were divided into age groups and then into weight groups. I was in the group for 12- and 13-year-olds who weighed 90 pounds. I was glad I didn't have to wrestle any boys who were bigger and older than I was.

There were charts on the wall that showed who would be wrestling together. The charts looked like this:

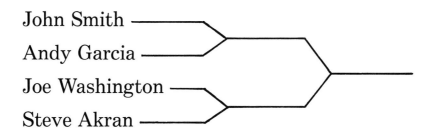

John Smith
Andy Garcia
Joe Washington
Steve Akran

Mr. Arnold told me how the chart worked. "You will wrestle the boy whose name is linked to your name. The winner's name will then go on the next line to the right. This winner will wrestle the winner of Joe's and Steve's match. When you lose, your name is dropped from the chart. But if you keep winning, your name will keep moving to the right."

There were so many wrestlers that I had
to wait for my first match. I watched the
other boys wrestle as I waited for my name
to be called. I was not as nervous as the
first time I had wrestled. I felt confident. I
was in good shape. And I had been working
hard to prepare for this tournament.

Finally my name was called. I went to the center of the mat and met my opponent. I thought I would be able to beat him. But I also remembered what everyone had told me: "Don't be overconfident. Don't underestimate the ability of your opponent."

The first match was very tiring. I had the chance to try out moves that I had never used before. I worked and worked, but I could not pin my opponent. He was stronger than I thought he would be.

When the match was over, I had won by a score of 8 to 6. That was one of the happiest moments of my life.

My parents took me out to lunch to help celebrate. I did not eat much because I had to wrestle again that afternoon.

I was confident at the start of my second match. I remembered my first match. I liked how it felt to win.

Almost from the time the whistle blew to start the match, I knew I was in trouble. My opponent was really good. Even though I could usually escape from him without too much trouble, he kept taking me down. Each time he did this, the score kept getting bigger and bigger . . . for him!

Finally the match was over. It was the longest and the hardest three minutes I had ever worked. My opponent beat me by a score of 14 to 10.

I was out of the tournament. But I stayed and watched the rest of the matches. At the end of the tournament, the judges gave out awards. The first, second, and third place winners in each age and weight group won big trophies.

Because I had lost, I did not think I would get a trophy. But the judges called out a list of names, and mine was on it. I received a small trophy to show that I had participated in the tournament.

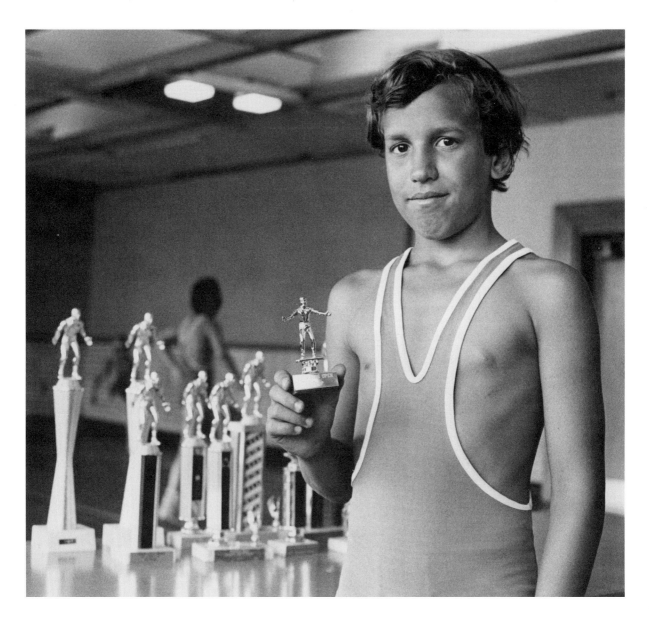

Well, that's my story. Wrestling season is over for this year, but I won't forget all of the things I learned and the friends I made. Next year, I'm going to start working out earlier so that I'll be ready for the whole season with the team. I've decided that wrestling is for me.